"Chip Bell has delivered a magnificent encore. Sprinkles *is chock-full of his* signature stories mixed with practical guidance.

—**Mark Pizzi, president, Nationwide Insurance**

"Luxury brands require luxury service. Sprinkles *is a delightful treasure for all who care about taking service to a pinnacle level.*"

—**Doug Kindy, president, Lucchese Boot Company**

"Chip Bell has prepared another entertaining book with a giant helping of creative ways to transform good-to-great service into unique and distinctive service.*"

—**Marshall Goldsmith, *New York Times* bestselling author of *Mojo***

"Sprinkles *will bring infectious joy to all who read it and powerful results to all who apply it.*"

—**Tariq Farid, founder and CEO, Edible Arrangements**

"Innovative service takes a bold mix of a maverick spirit, a commitment to your customer, and provocative thinking and actions. Chip Bell's book shows you the best way to create and serve that special blend to get extraordinary business results.*"

—**Carol Roth, "Recovering" Investment Banker, entrepreneur, CNBC contributor, and *New York Times* bestselling author**

"Whether customers expect your relationship to be sparkly or, like me, just plain nuts, my friend Chip Bell's book will help you deliver on their ever-evolving expectations."

—Jim Blasingame, host of "The Small Business Advocate Show"
and author of *The Age of the Customer*

"*Sprinkles* is the recipe for inspiring experiences that get customers talking. The stories will enchant you, the insights will instruct you, and the techniques will improve your service."

—Farmer Lee Jones, cofounder of The Chef's Garden

"Chip Bell promises a 'delicious journey to innovative service,' and wow, does he deliver! While it's important to get the basics right, in *Sprinkles* he brings to life another truth—customers also crave unique and pleasurable experiences."

—Bob Thompson, founder and CEO of CustomerThink
and author of *Hooked On Customers*

"*Sprinkles* is another entertaining and insightful book from master storyteller, Chip Bell. I suspect that Chip may be distantly related to Sherlock Holmes as he has an uncanny ability to discover great service and to draw out conclusions that most of us would surely overlook."

—Eva Niewiadomski, Ranch Czarina, Catalyst Ranch

SPR NKLES

CREATING **AWESOME EXPERIENCES**

THROUGH **INNOVATIVE SERVICE**

CHIP R. BELL

GREENLEAF
BOOK GROUP PRESS

Published by Greenleaf Book Group Press
Austin, Texas
www.gbgpress.com

Distributed by Greenleaf Book Group

For ordering information or special discounts for bulk purchases, please contact
Greenleaf Book Group at PO Box 91869, Austin, TX 78709, 512.891.6100.

Design, cover design, and composition by Greenleaf Book Group
Image credits: ©iStockphoto/shingopix (pile of sprinkles), ©Shutterstock/Ellen Mol, ©Shutterstock/Peshkov Daniil, ©Shutterstock/vrjoyner, ©Shutterstock/Alexander Tihonov, ©Shutterstock/alisafarov, ©Shutterstock/EwaPix, ©Shutterstock/Venus Angel, ©Shutterstock/romrf, ©Shutterstock/Artazum and Iriana Shiyan, ©Shutterstock/Catherine Murray, ©Shutterstock/focal point, ©Shutterstock/Dragon Images, ©Shutterstock/Michael C. Gray, ©Shutterstock/Undrey, ©Shutterstock/SmileStudio, ©Shutterstock/Chones, ©iStockphoto/shingopix (sprinkles spread out)
Customer Forensics® is a registered trademark of Chip R. Bell.

Cataloging-in-Publication data
Bell, Chip R.
  Sprinkles : creating awesome experiences through innovative service / Chip R. Bell.—First edition.
   pages : illustrations ; cm
  Issued also as an ebook.
  1. Customer services. 2. Creative ability in business. 3. Success in business. I. Title.

HF5415.5 .B45 2015
658.812   2014947623
ISBN 13: 978-1-62634-175-3

Part of the Tree Neutral® program, which offsets the number of trees consumed in the production and printing of this book by taking proactive steps, such as planting trees in direct proportion to the number of trees used: www.treeneutral.com

TreeNeutral

Printed in China

15 16 17 18 19 20   10 9 8 7 6 5 4 3 2 1

First Edition

TO NANCY

THE RECIPE FOR INNOVATIVE SERVICE

(a.k.a. the Table of Contents)

BE MY GUEST!

*"It is not the quantity of the meat, but the cheerfulness of
the guests, which makes the feast."*
—Edward Hyde

Welcome! I'm honored you elected to join me on a delicious journey to innovative service. Think of this book you're holding like a floating banquet. You know, the kind where you enjoy the appetizer at one friend's house, the salad at another home, and end the evening with dessert at the last house. This banquet we share will feature various approaches to delivering an unexpected, tantalizing experience to all you serve. It's all about a customer experience that is served gourmet style.

The origin of this book came from two sources. The first was a quote by Anthony Bourdain, celebrity chef and host of the TV show *Parts Unknown*. "Anyone who's a chef, who loves food, ultimately knows that all that matters is: 'Is it good? Does it give pleasure?'" Innovative service is a blend of these same two sentiments. As customers, we all want service that is good—meaning it successfully fulfills our needs or accomplishes the outcome we seek. But, we remember service that comes with an experience that gives us unexpected pleasure.

The second source for this book came from my three granddaughters, Kaylee, Annabeth, and Cassie. They taught me that a great cookie becomes a really special cookie only when adorned with sprinkles, icing, or a cherry. Service is the same. Customers want their experiences to be more than great . . . they want them special. As customers, we like great service; but we love service that takes our breath away—the kind that leaves us "awed" not just "wowed." This book is about how to deliver an experience as enchanting and memorable as a special cookie.

In 2013, I wrote *The 9½ Principles of Innovative Service*. The emotional response to that book from buyers, reviewers, and talk show hosts was very gratifying; it was also very revealing. The book gave readers the freedom and rationale for making service ingenious and creative, not just good or even great. It made frontline employees feel less like worker bees and more like fireflies.

Leaders of organizations have spent years focusing on delivering value-added service. Yet today's customers, with their inclination toward elevating their expectations every time a service provider adds more, have almost run the delivery of service delight straight into the too-pricey zone. Each time a service provider adds more in their effort to exceed customer expectations, it comes closer to completely eliminating profit margins already razor thin for most.

The new perspective reflected in both this book and *The 9½ Principles* is this: value-unique service and not value-added service provides a more promising path to delight—one with ingenuity, not addition. We all have unlimited ways to serve uniquely but only a finite number of ways to add more. My hope is the gourmet cooking metaphor will unleash fresh ideas and tasty techniques for delivering innovative service—the kind Bourdain spoke about: good, but also pleasurable enough for customers to remark about it to others.

Bottom line—this book is about your bottom line. Customers today crave special and unique. They are not only tired of ho-hum, they are bored with the "pretty-good-but-nothing-to-write-home-about" kind of service. When a large brokerage firm decided to have fun with their phone tree by adding "punch 8 to hear a duck quack," they were stunned when over a million people a week called just to hear the duck. The punch line? Customers want service à la mode. They gravitate toward people with spirit, organizations with imagination, and leaders with spunk. They want their service experiences delivered with sprinkles.

Get ready for a decadent banquet that will stretch your menu in new ways to serve with innovation. And, when you get to the dessert at the end, please drop mc a note to let me know what you thought of this gourmet recipe!

"Hospitality is making your guest feel at home,
even though you wish they were."

—Author Unknown

SERVE WITH INNOVATION

"Breakthroughs come from an instinctive judgment of what customers might want if they knew to think about it."
—Andrew Grove, former chairman and CEO, Intel

We met for breakfast in the restaurant of the antique Foshay Tower (now a W Hotel) in downtown Minneapolis. My breakfast guest was the renowned cartoonist John Bush. Now deceased, his syndicated cartoons were at that time white-hot. I was there to learn how his mind worked because my co-author, Ron Zemke, and I were in search of someone to illustrate our new business book.

"Let's sit at the table by the window so we can see the people in the street," he suggested after we met. When the waitress came to take our order, John had not even glanced at his menu. "Just bring me something out of the ordinary," John requested. The waitress started to tell him some of the more off-the-beaten-path menu items and John stopped her. "Just surprise me!" He made my two eggs over easy with toast and bacon seem plain vanilla!

After a few typical interview questions, I asked how he came up with cartoon ideas. "The cool ideas are everywhere," he said. "I just pick something and daydream about what it might be like. You have to let it work you as much as you are making it work."

"Give me an example," I probed. John smiled.

"Well, give me a subject . . . any subject . . . and let me see where it wants me to take it," John proposed. I was struck by how he spoke of ideas as if they were good friends with a mind of their own. "How about a cartoon about a dog?" I suggested. A man was at that moment walking by our street side window with a beagle hound on a leash. John took out his drawing pad like a kid opening a new box of crayons.

"Why don't we put the dog in a restaurant like this one, having breakfast with his new owner," John recommended with an obvious passion welling up in his countenance. As he began to draw, the woman at the table nearby ordered a cappuccino. "Aha," said John. "Let's have the dog drinking a cappuccino!" And with that, his drawing pen portrayed the dog with lots of steamed-milk foam on his mouth.

With a wide-eyed look of satisfaction he exclaimed, "Done! All we need is a caption; I think I have just the one!" He penciled in the lines the dog in the cartoon was speaking to his owner seated across from him at a restaurant table.

"My last owner wouldn't let me order this . . . said it made me look crazy!"

I howled. "That is hilarious," I said. But my quest for symmetry forced me to continue: "But, why not have the caption say . . . 'said it made me look mad?'" I got the best creativity lesson of all. "The creative part of humor," John stated, "is to let the viewer fill in the pattern. There would be little to 'get' if you made it totally obvious. It needs to pop in the viewer's mind like the punch line of a joke." We hired John Bush! He would ultimately illustrate several of our books on knock-your-socks-off service.

Gourmet service requires a dash of innovation . . . the application of creativity and ingenuity. Cooks follow the recipe; great chefs embellish, experiment, and use a lot of "suit to taste." But, you're not innovative or creative, you say? Perhaps you have just not been looking at the right source. What if you picked something random and applied it to your service experience? John Bush used a dog walking by.

What if you chose a different set of eyes to examine what you are seeking to solve? What would a group of first graders suggest? Or, a wonderful wizard? What would Walt Disney do? What if you turned your problem into a play, a food, an old movie, a celebration—the combinations are endless. What if you made your service experience smaller, done alone, done in reverse, done with a guide, greener, more romantic, slower, with elegance, easier, more inclusive, faster, done remotely—keep going!

Innovation comes from choosing the light . . . a sort of table by the window. When someone has a brilliant "Aha!" moment, we label it insight. It happens when you are placed in a position to experience energy in action and join with it. It is the result of focused daydreaming, letting reality blend with fantasy in a totally nonjudgmental manner. It surfaces when you are willing to take the risk to rearrange order and upset the tried (or tired) and true.

Innovation happens when you effortlessly ignore mind-limiting barriers and laugh at conventions that are mere form. It is there when you find joy in the simplicity of life and allow yourself to be completely awed. Become friends of the bizarre; partners with the uncommon. It happens when you relax with your issue and let it "play us" instead of seeking to control it. It appears when you engage others in the search—a customer, a colleague, or someone unrelated to your problem. Innovation happens when passion becomes the magical bond that links head and heart. Failure is merely feedback, never rejection.

There is a creative person inside each of us waiting to emerge and make service gourmet in an innovative way. John demonstrated a flow without a pause button. He showed an obvious excitement that he could be both spectator and creator, thus, marveling at the gift that was given to him to express. And, the ease with which he demonstrated his amazing genius loudly telegraphed that the gift was available for anyone willing to request a table by the window and freely play!

"Innovation doesn't come just from giving people incentives; it comes from creating environments where their ideas can connect."

—Steven Johnson

CHAPTER ONE

EVERYTHING GOES BETTER WITH SPRINKLES

"I doubt whether the world holds for anyone a more soul-stirring surprise than the first adventure with ice cream."
—Heywood Broun

It was late Thursday afternoon when I checked into the Ritz-Carlton in Atlanta. After a tough week on the road, this was clearly an elegant venue for my last stop. My dress pants needed pressing for my Friday morning keynote, so I dialed the hotel housekeeping department. I was told someone would be right up to get my pants.

Moments later, a tiny Asian women in her mid-fifties knocked on my door. Taking my pants she informed me she would have them back to me in less than an hour. Forty-five minutes later, she was back.

"Thank you for giving me the honor of pressing your beautiful pants," she said with an excited smile on her face. "This is the nicest pair of pants I think I have ever pressed." I wondered about the source of her gracious style and passionate attitude. What made Nuriya Mohsen so guest-centric?

"Here is my business card," she politely said. "Call me anytime and I will take care of your laundry needs." Her card revealed her job title: "Laundry/ Valet."

It was at that point she added sprinkles to my already great service. "And, on behalf of the Ritz-Carlton Buckhead, I would like to present you with this package of stays for your dress shirt collars." Now, think about it. How many hotel laundry employees on the planet have their own business card plus a special surprise gift to present to guests?

Unlike elegant icing or fancy cake decoration, sprinkles are not complex or arduous. They are super easy, random performances available to all of us all of the time. As a performance, they should be sprinkled on with deliberate abandon, much like a fairy with a wand. When the person in the vehicle in front of us pays our toll in the tollbooth, we tell people. When a departing customer gives our child their unused tickets as we arrive at the county fairground, we tell people. As customers, we are thankful for random acts of kindness. And, when those acts are totally unexpected, we are also talkative.

With three granddaughters aged six, eight, and ten, we keep a very large supply of sprinkles. You might say we are sprinkles experts! We have multicolored sprinkles, chocolate sprinkles, and heart-shaped sprinkles. There are sprinkles that look like colored dots and ones that look like tiny tubes. Sprinkles typically live their very short life on top of a cupcake or a cookie. But, if you see the world through our granddaughters' eyes, they belong on just about everything in life. Sprinkles adorn, enrich, enliven, and excite. Sprinkles make ice cream look like it was prepared by a clown, not a cook. They make pancakes seem prepared by a gourmet chef, not by a granddaddy!

What would your customer's service experience be like if it was sprinkled? Checkout clerks would shake your hand, not just say "hello." The newspaper delivery person would leave a thoughtful note tucked in your newspaper. Pizza delivery boxes would have funny faces inside waiting to greet you when the box was opened. The bank teller would give you an extra thousand in play money just to make you laugh. The reception area would look like the interior decorator got extra leeway. And, there would be fresh flowers in the middle of the boardroom table, not just water pitchers. Operators would have a humor in their voice, and flight attendants would offer you pink lemonade, not just soft drinks or water.

"I figured if I was going to make the world a better place, I'd do it with cookies," said *Stranger Than Fiction* character Ana Pascal. It is a powerful concept for innovative service. "Sprinkles" is code for any heartstring-plucking surprise that takes service from great to awesome. Paraphrasing famed restaurateur Danny Meyer, great service happens to you; innovative service happens for you.

When the only FirstBank & Trust ATM in the rural town of Tahoka, Texas, went down, customers were unhappy. They were forced to use the only other ATM in the area at a convenience store where fees were considerably higher.

And, when it took several weeks to get the ATM operative, unhappy customers were accustomed to going to the convenience store for their cash. FirstBank & Trust marketing executive Andy Hartman found a way to lure customers back to the bank's ATM—"sprinkles." He ran an ad in the local paper that told customers not to think it was a mechanical glitch if they received a fifty dollar bill instead of a twenty dollar bill when they used the bank's ATM. Word spread as customers told neighbors when they hit the ATM jackpot!

How can you deliver gourmet service with surprise? What if you treated every customer like today was his or her birthday? What would your service be like if it came with balloons, candy kisses, a chocolate coin, a funny one-liner, or popcorn? A hospital in Milwaukee asked new patients their favorite flower during admission. They then arranged for a single stem of that favorite flower be placed in a bud vase on the patient's bedstand. What would a spunky eight-year-old suggest you do? If the service experience you deliver became a super hero, how would it change? What would you do differently if you wanted your service experience to win the Cracker Jack Award for amazement?

THE SECRET SAUCE—AMAZEMENT

"I want a cookie" is a favorite request of most toddlers. Permissive parents give in; disciplined parents say something akin to "After you eat all your lunch!" Grandparents say, "How 'bout I get you two!" The cookie request in some ways becomes code for who can influence whom.

When a child hits five or six years old, this simple cookie request changes to the more theatrical "I *need* a cookie." Most parents spot the ploy and parry the child's request with something like "How about you *need* an apple instead." Most grandparents spot the ploy and couldn't care less!

Customers have always wanted customer delight. It was the sizzle that went with the steak; the cherry that went on top. We pointed to ways that Nordstrom was different than Sears, Disney World was different than Six Flags, or Amazon was different than Borders. But, customers have changed. Today, they need a cookie so to speak. They assume they will get a quality outcome or product at a fair price. And, they assume they will get good service. Without these features, they take their business elsewhere, leaving bad tweets, snarky YouTube videos, and poor reviews littered along their exit path.

The secret to differentiation today is amazement. And, everything a service provider can do to unexpectedly take customers' breath away moves them closer to ensnaring customers' hearts and completely ruining their appetite for any competitor.

"The moments of happiness we enjoy take us by surprise.
It is not that we seize them, but that they seize us."

—Ashley Montagu

CHAPTER TWO

MAKE PASSION
THE SPICE OF SERVICE

"Research tells us fourteen out of any

ten individuals likes chocolate."

—Sandra Boynton

I walked into the restaurant off the lobby of the Park Inn west of Harrisburg, PA. From the back of the restaurant I heard, "Good morning, how would you like your coffee?" When I said black, the voice warmly responded, "Take any table you like, and I'll have your coffee there before you can sit down!"

My day was off to a captivating start, like a colorful merry-go-round!

"I'm Sandy. Do I get the awesome pleasure of serving you today?" she asked as she laid my menu beside the cup of coffee she had already poured. The breakfast was perfect and served quickly. Periodically, Sandy checked to make sure all was well. There was no chitchat as I focused on my morning paper, just attentiveness . . . and lots of smiles aimed point-blank at my table. I finished, folded up my newspaper, and requested my check. It had been a joy to be served by someone noticeably passionate about customers. And then, it happened!

Sandy brought my check along with a go cup of black coffee! "This is great!" I exclaimed. "You have no idea how much I needed a coffee to go today." Sandy smiled, winked, and responded, "It's our gift to you!"

Folks, it does not get any better than that! I left her a tip almost as big as my breakfast tab and went straight to the manager on duty to compliment her over-the-top, high-spirited service. "I'm so delighted," he said, "but, I will tell you, we get comments about Sandy almost every day. In fact, we have guests who tell us they drive way out of their way just to get a shot of Sandy in the morning!"

Feisty service is as mischievous as April Fools' Day. It is service with panache and flair. Surprising service can be subtle and low-key; feisty is always assertive and bubbly. And, it is a potent fertilizer that can cultivate customer growth. If you want something to grow, pour champagne on it! Think of feisty as the champagne of gourmet service and the perfect antidote to spirit leeches. And what's a spirit leech?

One of the hazards of fishing swampy rivers is the risk of getting a leech. Unlike many parasites, you cannot feel a leech attaching to your arm or leg. A ritual among river anglers is to always check for the bloodsuckers after emerging from the water. And, the typical way to remove the slimy hitchhiker is with a lighted match or lighter.

Leeches suck the blood from their target; spirit leeches suck the energy and passion from theirs. Some spirit leeches are dark—they remove optimism, hope, and confidence. Mention an opportunity, and they can tell you why it's a mistake. Suggest a new approach to resolving a problem, and they will tell you all the reasons it won't work. Some are transparent, preying on personal accountability. They play the blame game or bring out the excuse use. Some are almost invisible, specializing in putting wet blankets on joy.

Spirit leeches are removed the same way real leeches are—with fire. Not a lighted match, of course, but with the warmth and energy of a passionate, feisty spirit. Sandy would make even the most ornery customer feel valued. You do not inherit, acquire, or borrow a feisty spirit. You choose it much like you choose to introduce yourself to a stranger. Those who opt for upbeat decline to let spirit leeches attach to them. And, even introverts can muster up enough obvious passion to produce a customer grin!

When my business partner and I exited the Hertz courtesy van at the Hartford airport, the strong below-freezing winter wind bit hard. But, the Hertz attendant had a warm smile and an eager-to-help attitude. "This is way too cold!" one of us commented. She almost giggled. "Now, you guys know in Hartford we do weather as entertainment!" Ten miles down the road, we were still laughing at her unexpected champagne comment.

Feisty people rebuff the idea of being a slave to ritual. This does not mean they are rebellious or reckless. They know that breaking "the way we've always done it" norm can lead to enrichment, growth, and progress. They have learned that the pursuit of remarkable means continuous improvement and experimentation. Feisty rattles the status quo and upsets the civility of adequate and normal.

Pretend the service you deliver was a jack-in-the-box. How could you make it feel colorful? What are ways you can create a sense of anticipation . . . a buildup before the actual delivery. What is your service drumroll? And, what would make it so unexpected it makes your customer laugh or grin? Are there ways you can tease your customer in a warm and friendly way? Is there a "souvenir" you could bundle with the experience that would be a delayed delight when your customer later discovered it? A week after my wife bought a new car, she discovered the service tech had programmed in her radio stations from her trade-in and just let her discover it! Give your service punch and your customers will give you profits!

THE SECRET SAUCE—ANIMATION

Customers are attracted to spirited people! And, today's customers are frustrated with indifferent service—not bad service, just boring, comatose service. They witness service people sleepwalking through the workday. And, as they guard their ever-diminishing dollars, employee spirit is one component of value they carefully watch. When they witness employees who act like there is no light on inside, they are fast to flee with their funds.

Smart organizations nurture spirit. It is not about organizational loyalty anymore. We know that the days of employees saluting the company flag are long gone. It is about employees showing aliveness and enthusiasm while at work. Most organizations today would rather have a fired-up employee for a couple of years than endure an uninspired one who stays for the gold watch.

However, the very nature of spirit is to be unpredictable and untidy. The heart is more unruly than the head. And, "organization" can become the enemy of spirit. While there must be a balance between enthusiasm and efficiency, the rational side of enterprise has always had the upper hand. Are logical processes rendering your employees apathetically automatic? If mechanical wins over inventive and robotic replaces zealous, then the excitement customers adore will be wrung out of the organization. Where are the spirit leeches in your organization? How can they be exorcised?

"Nothing is so contagious as enthusiasm."

—Samuel Taylor Coleridge

CHAPTER THREE

ALWAYS ADD AN EXTRA HELPING

"True generosity is an offering; given freely and out of pure love.
No strings attached. No expectations."

—Suze Orman

Gem mining is a fun route to a granddaughter's heart. We had our three granddaughters for the weekend and took them gem mining in the North Georgia mountains. Granted the buckets of sand are previously salted with semiprecious stones collectively worth less than the ten dollars you pay for each bucket. But, that is not a "truth-in-mining" fact a six-year old cares to hear about.

The gem-mining place we chose was a mineshaft of innovative service. The exterior was littered with bright colored rocks promising a likely successful find on the other side of their front door. The tiny shop had lots of rock displays and gemstones set in jewelry. Our granddaughters' eyes were as large as mining pans. Then came an unexpected marvel—the storeowner's grey cat stuck its head through a baseball-sized hole in the ceiling above the girls. It was so surreal each girl wanted to be lifted up to touch it just to make certain the purring cat was not just some clever trick.

Once set up with a screen-covered frame, a bucket of sand, and a bench seat in front of a narrow water trough, the girls began their hunt for gems. Shaking the sand through the screen to unveil bright colored stones unleashed joy-filled squeals. The owner offered a quick geology class on each stone—amethyst, quartz, garnet, peridot, citrine, etc. Like a world-class tutor, she was patient and noticeably well-informed. Before leaving, we let the girls pick out one large piece of colored art glass in their birthstone color. Hundreds of art glass pieces lined long display tables, making the selection much like a treasure hunt.

Now, here is the best part. After every girl was completely satisfied with her choice, the owner asked, "And, what is grandmother's birth month?" When my wife said, "June," the owner momentarily disappeared only to return with a gorgeous piece of deep purple art glass (for the birthstone, Alexandrite). "This is yours," she said, "for being so nice to me and bringing your grandchildren to my gem store."

Gourmet service comes with an abundance of generosity. You "add" generosity, like you add a decoration. It is experienced as a gift, not a ploy. Cracker Jack could have sold its caramelized popcorn in their really cool looking box without a free prize inside. Zappos could have shipped its products to you using two-day UPS and not next-morning delivery at no extra charge. Disney World housekeepers could have cleaned your hotel room without turning a hand towel into a charming figure. Like the gem mine lady (as she became known in our family), the spirit of innovative service is all about a generous purple piece of glass at a tiny roadside gem store.

Generous service can also work when sprinkled on someone or something important to your customer. "What's your puppy's name?" makes any dog owner light up. "You sure have a cute daughter." can make a mother at the checkout counter smile despite having just gone through the challenge of managing a three-year-old in a grocery store. "What a cool looking set of wheels!" can turn even the meanest looking road hog into a bowl of jelly.

"Amy's Plant" has a special meaning to a good friend of mine. And, it always makes him smile whenever you ask him about it. But, I am getting way ahead of myself!

My good friend tore down a shed in his side yard. The ugly old shed was in stark contrast with the rest of his highly coiffured lawn. He decided to turn the space into a flower garden complete with a lattice-covered sitting area. When it came time to purchase plants and ornamental trees, he took along his six-year-old granddaughter, Amy. The salesperson at the nursery treated Amy as a part of the decision-making process . . . to the delight of my friend. Amy got to be the salesperson's helper, and he even asked her opinion on some of the plants.

Amy was over at her granddaddy's house the afternoon the plants and trees were delivered. After all were placed in the spots where they would be planted, the driver had one more plant to unload. It was a small, aromatic rosemary plant with a tag that read, "Amy's plant." She was thrilled and got to personally choose the spot where it would be planted. Now, every time she visits Paw Paw, she races to the side yard to check on the growth of *her* plant.

Whenever someone visits my friend's garden, or seeks his input on a good place to buy plants, or asks about any topic even remotely related to horticulture, that inquirer will get to hear the "Amy's Plant" story. Don't wait for your customers to wear an "Ask Me About My Granddaughter" button. Find ways to learn the target of their affinity and add it to your list as well.

THE SECRET SAUCE—ABUNDANCE

Allowances were not something my dad believed taught kids a work ethic. So, I worked for all my spending money. Living in a rural area, the only paying chores for kids were babysitting and lawn mowing. My sister babysat; I mowed yards. I got a dollar for a regular-sized yard and two dollars for a large yard; my grandmother had a two-dollar yard!

One summer we had a drought. Yards did not grow much, so I was looking at a pretty bleak school year in terms of spending money. Toward the end of that summer, my grandmother called and wanted me to come mow her yard. I was thrilled! As always, I mowed her yard and met her on her back porch to get my two dollars. But, I got a big surprise. She handed me a five dollar bill and said the most wonderful words . . . "Keep the change!" And, it did change my relationship with my grandmother. A relationship I *kept* until she died in her mid-eighties.

One powerful route to your customer's heart is an abundant attitude—the type that leaves customers surprised, not just happy. Now, few organizations can provide customers with a 150 percent tip like my grandmother. While the economics of a ten-year-old's piggybank are important, it was her abundance mentality that created the warm memory of our relationship.

A generous attitude has a magnetic impact on customers. It attracts them because it conveys to the customer the kind of unconditional positive regard that characterizes relationships at their best. Customers like the way they feel when dealing with service providers who have such an orientation. They feel valued, not used. They enjoy relationships laced with substance and value far more than encounters that are functional, but hollow. In the words of Judith Olney, "Always serve too much hot fudge sauce on hot fudge sundaes."

"There are no traffic jams along the extra mile."

—Roger Staubach

CHAPTER FOUR

PUT A CHERRY ON TOP OF GREAT SERVICE

*"Happiness is life served up with a scoop of acceptance,
a topping of tolerance, and sprinkles of hope,
although chocolate sprinkles also work."*
—Robert Brault

Let's try a fun exercise based on a real situation. You look for all the places a cherry could have gone on top of this experience.

I had lunch at a well-known seafood restaurant chain. The seafood was good and reasonably priced. There were a few nautical photos on the walls.

Except for those two features—pictures and menu—it could have just as easily been a steakhouse or Italian food restaurant. I left without any thought of the seaside on my mind. But, I could not help but notice the wide array of missed opportunities to turn a pleasant meal into a powerful memory. So, what would you do with this seafood restaurant? Here are some of my observations; you identify how it could be more "sensory."

The landscaping out front was very similar to the nearby Chili's rocks and cacti. The hostess greeted me with, "Welcome to Fish Feast" (not their real name). The music playing was Vince Gill. And, the place smelled like any family restaurant, not one with a particular theme. The waitress was nice and wore a white logoed shirt, but no uniform or costume. When I asked her about the tilapia, she only knew how it was prepared, but she couldn't tell me any more specific characteristics of the fish—like its texture, or where it was caught.

Their silent bathroom could have been exported from any medium-priced restaurant in the country. The place mat was colorful—blues and greens, but without pictures or puzzles or "little-known facts." And, my take-away souvenir after paying the bill? A toothpick that tasted like wood; not even salty. The receipt was the same color as the one I get at a Wal-Mart checkout. So, how would you make this restaurant colorful to all the senses?

Scenography originated in ancient Greece. Artists painted colorful stage scenes on stones for theatrical productions. Colorful service involves integrating all the sensory elements of a service experience so they are congruent around a compelling story, theme, or vision. The secret is attention to minute details because the customer's brain can pick up any dissonant signal or symbol.

We humans favor symmetry. Our psyche reads dissonance in an experience long before our logical mind comprehends a reason. Far more than the urge to level a crooked picture or the recognition that something is off on the melody we hear, dissonance reaches even to ideas out of alignment with our beliefs.

The scenography of service can be your playground to choreograph the total mindset of your customers. Put your senses on steroids and create an experience that yields a story your customers are eager to spread. Gourmet service is colorfully congruent. It delights our subconscious in a way our wide-awake mind might not even comprehend. Let's examine a great illustration of sensory service.

A joule is a measure of energy. The Joule is a place of happy energy. The upscale boutique hotel in downtown Dallas has made happy energy (the Chinese call it "chi") its main attraction physically, emotionally, and spiritually. There are many reasons the hotel has earned a five-star distinction! Let's take a peak at their sensory service.

Arrive at The Joule and an upbeat doorman escorts you to the front desk where he introduces you to the clerk rather than announcing you. It is the kind of hosting in which a handshake is in order. The attitude of "yes" permeates every person in the property. The lobby has a superlong, narrow banquet table with lots of chairs along each side and stacks of interesting books as the entree. A giant wheel constantly turns in the lobby like a gristmill turning corn into meal. The tenth-floor pool provocatively extends eight feet beyond the hotel's structure, giving swimmers the sensation of swimming right off the edge of the building.

Guest rooms are appointed with a bathroom sink that reminds you of a small waterfall from a purple hillside. All room lighting is mood enabled. The colors richly embrace you as you enter the bedroom. The office section of guest rooms feels like a real office complete with accessible outlets, Aeron office chair, and adjustable desk. The hotel restaurant off the lobby—CBD Provisions—echoes the same happy, carefree energy from its sound, smell, and ambiance to its menu items—pan-roasted quail, little goat pie, pig tails, and grapefruit pie.

After a wonderful stay, I checked out of the hotel with a big smile that I passed on to the doorman, and to the taxi driver, and to the airport TSA agent, and to the airline gate attendant, and to the . . . ! The word joule is a word pronounced the same as jewel, and like a precious stone, this hotel offers a delectable and enriching experience to everyone who crosses its threshold.

When realtors suggest baking an apple pie before holding an open house, when cookie shops pipe their kitchen aroma onto the sidewalk, and when upscale retail stores put a pianist at a baby grand on the sales floor, all are declaring the common sense of uncommon senses. What opportunities would you discover if you looked at your own unit or organization through your scenographic eyes?

Know your customers well, and aim for the response you believe your customers value. Consider the emotion and sensations (real or imagined) you want to call to mind, but also pay close attention to those sense triggers that clash with your desired response and chase them away. Does that picture on the wall really add value? Are the restrooms compatible and congruent with the rest of your strategy? When was the last time you examined your parking lot, waiting area, or front entrance with a focus on sensory signals being conveyed? What should customers see first, second . . . last? How are key service transitions managed? Is there distracting background noise when customers call your business?

THE SECRET SAUCE—AMBIANCE

The effective use of sense cries not just for congruence but also for creativity. Take it from Billy Rivera of Karaoke Cab in Charlotte, who was the subject of a story by Simone Orendain on the NPR news program *All Things Considered* for his novel approach to a mundane service. With a laptop in the front seat next to him and a screen scrolling the words on the back of the seat that the passengers can view, he offers customers a choice of over 39,000 songs. Some passengers so enjoy the wild sing-a-long, they ask Billy to keep driving around the block until the song ends, not minding that the meter continues to run.

Think about what associations might be caused by each sense attraction you consider. Sights, sounds, and smells are all cues for customers that can surface pleasant or not-so-pleasant memories. A sign with red lettering might send a different message than the same sign in green. Once you have decided on the senses to appeal to, find ways to introduce them in a way that customers discover and delight in. Also remember that sensory enhancement must reflect proportion and balance. If your customers are singing along with the music, it might be playing too loud.

The very essence of innovative service is indulgent, decorated service. If service were an attraction, great service would be Disney World; innovative service would be Cirque du Soleil. It means stirring the soul while meeting a need. Gourmet chefs focus on presentation not just on preparation. Your customers deserve the same!

"A great chef is a mixture of artistry and craft."

—Wolfgang Puck

CHAPTER FIVE

GIVE THE GREATEST THING
SINCE SLICED BREAD

*"The only ones among you who will be really happy are those
who will have sought and found how to serve."*
—Albert Schweitzer

Charlie was the doorman at the Marriott Quorum hotel in Dallas and was legendary throughout the Marriott Corporation. After I heard Bill Marriott mention Charlie during a fireside chat with a group of Marriott senior leaders whom I was teaching at an off-site retreat, I had to interview Charlie. The belief was that Charlie knew the names of thousands of guests. He had already worked many years beyond the point most employees would have taken their pension and gone fishing.

When I asked the obvious question—Why do you keep doing this?—his answer was profound. "I am here for the love," he told me quietly. "When I love my guests by giving them my very best, they give it right back to me. Frankly, I am here for what they do for me." There is no greater gift one can give a customer than delivering service painted the color of love. But, it is more than just the love of the customer, as Charlie described.

"I love sprinkles so much," said Annabeth, my middle granddaughter, her words muffled with a mouth full of cupcake. Then, she added a comment filled with the wisdom only a child could muster. "And, I am sure this cupcake loves having them too." When we think of service passion, we generally think only of the Charlie-type love in motion—a service person's passion for the customer. But, real passion also goes to the "cupcake." It is the service person's love for the product or service they represent.

I had just finished a keynote to a group of salespeople for a large Caterpillar dealership. One participant quickly made his way to the front of the ballroom to take issue with my advice to show customers how much you love getting to serve them. "That ain't me," he said. "I'm not a 'show people I love 'em' kinda guy." Before I could answer, the CEO of the dealership, who had been standing nearby and heard the man's concern, said, "Then, Tom, just show them how much you love a CAT dirt pan or bulldozer and your customer will get it."

Shwetha loves HP! No, that's not a carving on a school ground tree or a Krylon spray painting on a water tower or overpass. Shwetha is a support tech operator for Hewlett-Packard. And, her style, behavior, and words clearly display her devotion to the HP brand she fronts.

I had purchased a new MacBook Air that was souped up with Windows 8.1 and Office 13. While I have a new HP color printer, my old, reliable workhorse printer is a monochrome HP LaserJet P2015dn. Not only is this printer a veritable antique as printers go, it has been out of warranty for years. I was only able to find a universal printer driver for my new laptop to talk to the printer. It allowed me to print, but not print front and back like the printer did with my old laptop. I finally surrendered and gave HP Technical Support an evening call.

I hit the jackpot! I got Shwetha! She was warm, clear, and patient. She informed me that because my HP printer was out of warranty there would normally be a charge for her technical services. But, she really wanted me to have a good experience with my HP and was willing to help me without a charge. We began troubleshooting. She was noticeably passionate about the product and my success with it. After numerous tests, we learned I had not checked the proper computer port in my printer setup. With that, she made it work perfectly.

Now, let me ask you a question. If you really, really loved a product or service, you would want to make sure it was delivering perfectly, right? Shwetha closed our conversation with, "May I call you back tomorrow just to make sure you are happy with how your HP printer is working?" Let me remind you this was a free call on an out-of-warranty product . . . a call driven solely by the deep brand allegiance of a call center tech rep. It was as if my old printer had actually been crafted by Shwetha herself. The next day she called just as she promised. And, her love affair with HP got passed on to me. I would never own any other brand!

Where does service with adoration come from? It comes from ensuring that the front line knows the brand's benefits, not just its features. It comes from investing in product/service employee education. If you're a leader, it comes from modeling the love for the brand you want employees to display. It involves making sure employees get to see the new ads before they are aired to the public. If you work for Ford, drive a Ford!

What can you do to make your customers fall in love with the service your unit or organization provides? Make a pledge to start the love connection with your next customer. Ignore the past, raise your hopes to greater plains, and make it happen. You know that affection is infectious. People smile at you and what do you do? You smile back. A stranger waves at you and you acknowledge their greeting. Passion (Pass-I-on) is a way of getting revenge against a challenging, difficult, and often indifferent world. So, go infect someone with your love of customers and love of the product or service you represent.

THE SECRET SAUCE—ADORATION

Mr. Hightower's cattle farm was adjacent to our family cattle farm in rural Georgia. Cattle farms were comprised of large grazing pastures; their inhabitants confined by unreliable metal fences. Cows generally escaped their incarceration when an elderly tree expired and fell across the fence. For some reason our cows always ventured north to Mr. Hightower's front lawn; his cows loitered south along the highway beside our pasture to visit our cows.

The manner my dad handled a Hightower cow invasion and how Mr. Hightower handled the exact same scenario was a powerful lesson in service with love. Mr. Hightower called up at first light with a demanding, "Ray, a bunch of your #%@ cows are out again! Get your boys up right now and come get 'em out of my front yard. They've probably eaten my squash." Mr. Hightower always forgot cows don't eat vegetables.

When my dad spotted Mr. Hightower's cows taking a joy ride, he never called. He calmly got us up to go with him to return the cows to their proper domicile. But, he went one step further. He found the site of their prison break and repaired it. He waited until he saw Mr. Hightower on Saturday uptown to provide a cordial briefing of the incident. Mr. Hightower never expressed gratitude and always seemed puzzled. But, it never mattered to my dad. He knew he had done a good deed, helped retain civility between neighbors, and taught his boys the power of service given with love.

"I would rather have thirty minutes of wonderful
than a lifetime of nothing special."

—Shelby Latcherie in *Steel Magnolias*

CHAPTER SIX

CUSTOMERS ENJOY BORROWING A CUP OF SUGAR

"Nothing makes you more tolerant of a neighbor's noisy party than being there."
—Franklin P. Jones

I stopped by a roadside flea market in search of an antique typewriter. "Your license plate is about to fall off," the owner told me as I was getting out of my car. I looked and saw the screw on the right side of the plate was about to come off. Handing me a Phillips screwdriver from his pile of used tools, he said, "Tighten that bad boy back up again before you lose it!" When I returned his screwdriver, he smiled and waved me away. "Just keep it, neighbor, I got plenty of them!" I thought to myself, "How long has it been since a merchant I had never seen before referred to me as 'neighbor'?" I vowed to come back, even after I located my typewriter.

Our fast-paced, get-it-on-the-Internet culture has stripped out much of the neighbor-serving-neighbor service experience. And, when we get that special neighborly experience, it makes us feel special with a nostalgic sense of being home. It requires caring about the person, not just the customer's request or requirement. It includes displaying the upbeat attitude you hope your customers will assume. It means never letting customers get out of your eyesight or earshot still disappointed. Even if you can't always give customers what they want, you can always give them a great service experience.

The night before my annual physical examination, I received a text from my physician reminding me that the morning exam would be started with a blood test. "Remember, no food after midnight and only water or black, unflavored coffee in the morning." I am a big coffee fan! As soon as the nurse took two vials of blood the next morning, she stepped out for a second and returned with a large cup of coffee. "I believe you like your coffee black," she said with a smile on her face . . . "and hazelnut, right?" She had gone to the Keurig coffee machine in their break area. Nurse Melody became Saint Melody. I felt like a member of their family!

What makes innovative service neighborly is the large portion of trust mixed into the brew. Trust comes through relationships. What makes service different than product is the presence of feeling, not just form. While we expect every Model 423B trash compactor from the same manufacturer to be identical, we know the next cashier will not be a carbon copy of the last. As customers, we admire the absence of variance in products; we find that same trait in service to be robotic and mechanical. We like our products uniform, but we want our service unique—crafted just for us.

This reality underscores the power of trust homemade by people. Homemade trust is fashioned through the small acts of communication and caring that make customers feel every service person is on their team, not on the opposition's squad. When the mechanic takes the time to explain all of your car repair options—from the cheaper quick fix to the more expensive long-term solution, without trying to "cross-sell" you on a list of other needed repairs they just happened to discover while under the hood—it reminds us of that trust. When the pilot takes the time to explain why your plane has sat on the tarmac fifteen minutes past its scheduled departure, it begins to build a relationship of trust.

Neighborhood Cleaners on Lake Oconee has been my dry cleaner for a few years. Like all great dry cleaners, they pick up and deliver if you prefer. They are as ecologically sensitive as they are interpersonally friendly. They'll do off-the-beaten-path requests like fix a tear, hem a skirt, or Scotchguard your sofa pillow covers. They also do great recovery if there is a service hiccup.

One time, one of their cleaning machines got rebellious and ripped a hole in my pricey dress pants. They reimbursed me the original cost of the pants along with providing world-class mea culpa. But, they went beyond the call of duty by sending my pants to an expert tailor who returned them to an "almost like new" state—on the house!

But, the best part is their propensity to deliver an unexpected surprise with an extra shot of generosity. We were having breakfast at a local diner down the street from the dry cleaner's. At a nearby table sat the owner/operator of

Neighborhood Cleaners, Gene Thurston. We exchanged pleasantries. He finished his meal and left before we got our check. When we asked for our check, the waitress informed us that Gene had picked up the tab, including our tip! They may crack a button or hang instead of fold a dress shirt once in a while, but I would never consider another dry cleaner.

Take a page from the innovative approach used by the manager of the First Watch Restaurant in Overland Park, KS. He purchased a large supply of umbrellas for his customers. Attaching his business card to each one, he put them in a large container at the front door along with a sign that read: "If you need an umbrella, please take one. If you bring it back, we'll give you a free cup of coffee." Serve every customer as if you were serving your best friend. Authentic trumps ostentatious; thoughtful takes precedent over showy. Look for ways to make service feel sincerely homemade, not conveniently store-bought.

THE SECRET SAUCE—ALLEGIANCE

What is it about trust that makes customers feel valued? In part, it communicates that one-half of a relationship is reaching out to the other half. In the middle of the word "trust" is the word "us." Our allegiance to another (whether person, unit, or organization) is elevated when we experience their faith in us; when we sense they assume the best in us. Customers who are trusted tend to become ex officio members in your sales department. It takes focusing on the relationship value, not exclusively zeroing in on the transaction cost.

Stanley Marcus, founder of Neiman Marcus in Dallas, enjoyed telling the story of the young debutante who returned a $150 evening gown after one evening's rough treatment and wanted her money back. "It was obvious her own reckless behavior had left the dress in shambles," Marcus said. "But I gave her back her money. And in 1935, one hundred fifty dollars was a lot of money for a dress. But not only did she spend thousands of dollars with me over the next thirty years, she made sure all her wealthy friends did likewise. Trusting her turned out to be a great investment."

The trusting organization that treats customers like valued neighbors puts more focus on nurturing the relationship than miserly squeezing every dollar out of every transaction. This does not mean "giving away the shop." Everyone in the organization should protect and grow the assets of the organization.

However, customers truly cherish those organizations that refrain from "nickel and diming them to death." Look for opportunities to say "no charge" or "that one is on us." Find ways to do unexpected, extra favors for customers. And, just like the complimentary screwdriver at the flea market, it is the small, personalized extras that gain loyalty mileage, not the big, splashy ones.

"Faith is not belief without proof,
but trust without reservations."

—Elton Trueblood

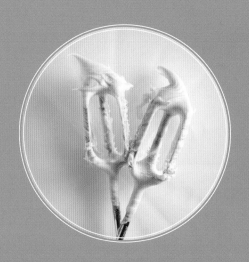

CHAPTER SEVEN

LET YOUR CUSTOMERS "LICK THE BEATERS"

"People will care when they share."

In the early 1950s, Betty Crocker was on a roll. The company's twenty-year successful advertising run of Bisquick ("90 seconds from package to oven") clearly positioned the company as the partner to homemakers eager to make meal preparation quick and easy. The company (owned by General Mills) elected to expand into cake mixes with the introduction of White Cake in 1951. It was a mix that simply required adding water, exactly like Bisquick.

However, the product failed to take off. Housewives felt no need to brag about their "made from scratch" biscuits or pancakes. But, cakes were different. After all, the colorful box promised a "fresh, homemade quality." When the company removed the powdered eggs from the mix and had the home-maker add real eggs, the product took off. The message: customers care more when they are given an invitation to put skin in the game.

"Licking the Beaters" is a familiar occurrence when kids are invited to assist in dessert making. And, as a youngster you felt bold and daring when you got to eat raw cookie dough. The symbolism is instructive for when and how to include customers in the creation of an experience. Customers care when they share . . . particularly if sharing is invited, not expected; when positioned as an adventure, not as an encumbrance or guilt trip.

Customer inclusion begins by being comfortable enough to ask the customer for assistance. It also means being willing at times to sacrifice a bit on efficiency or effectiveness for the commitment gained by participation. When customers are invited to assist, the path they take may not be identical to the one you would take or expect. Like effective delegation, the delegator must exchange some control for cooperation.

Avoid any customer request that makes the organization or customer in any way liable or puts either at risk if things go wrong. While the goal is to help the customer feel like a member of the family, it is important to remember the customer is always the guest of the organization. Preface your request with a simple statement: "I need your help," or a simple question: "May I ask of you a small favor?" Simplicity and sincerity are important tunes and tones to help the customer get with the rhythm of partnership. And, remember, some customers want to be pampered, not partnered. They would be insulted if you suggested they do more than give you their money.

The Seven Principles of Customer Inclusion

1. Only ask for what is reasonable—a request appropriate to make of a loyal customer.
2. Make the request the way your mother taught . . . the "may I" and "please" courtesies we learned growing up.
3. Provide customers with a brief background when making a request for assistance.

4. Requests for customer participation must contain the element of choice.

5. Make certain the customer sees participation as a collective effort.

6. Give the customer plenty of breathing room.

7. Never forget to express your gratitude.

Hurricane Hugo came ashore near Charleston, South Carolina, and was still a hurricane when it hit Charlotte, some 200 miles inland. It caused an unexpected crowd at Myers Park Hardware in Charlotte, as customers rushed to purchase candles, propane gas, chain saws, flashlight batteries, and other emergency supplies. The storeowner had limited help because her staff had been unable to get into work. She turned to her patrons for help.

I was standing nearby when I overheard storeowner Jo Huntington pull three frequent customers aside with these words: "Guys, have you ever thought about what it would be like to single-handedly save a store? Well, have I got a deal for you! If you have the time, I need you to help me run checkout."

When the guys donned their hardware store aprons and started bagging merchandise and ringing up sales, the crowd of formerly frustrated customers suddenly broke out in applause. These "volunteers" also registered their pleasure with the scene by offering to give up their "helper" slot to the highest bidder. It became a bit like Tom Sawyer convincing his skeptical onlookers that whitewashing a fence was an honor only for the carefully chosen and lucky few!

Customer inclusion is tangible evidence the relationship is egalitarian and valued. It signals an interdependence that elevates loyalty. Granted, there are customers who simply want to be served with no requirement to get involved. But, most customers enjoy being treated as a partner, not just as a consumer . . . especially when that invitation is issued with respect and completely voluntary. Let your customers help you co-create your next service delivery by giving them the best part . . . like the service version of getting to lick the beaters after helping to make a cake.

THE SECRET SAUCE—ALLIANCE

Matt Garofaio, owner of the Oconee Cellar near Lake Oconee in Georgia, decided to have a well-known bourbon brewery in Kentucky create a signature bourbon for him to sell in his upscale store. The brewery concocted five different distinctive options and sent them to Matt, each in a clear, numbered bottle the size of an old-fashioned cough syrup bottle. Now, how do you think Matt chose his special brand of nectar? He invited his best customers to taste test each of the five bourbons and register their preference. So, how many customers do you think will place orders for their "co-created" beverage?

The alliance of service provider with customers captivates because it is a clear and present reminder that providing a service always carries a co-created experience. Even if the experience is self-service, under the veneer of buttons and clicks is the personality of its designer. Too often, service providers forget that tantamount to a delightful, memorable experience is its egalitarian feature. Treating customers like "just consumers" and not partners disrespects the other half of the relationship while dishonoring the very essence of an implied covenant to fairly exchange value for value.

Smart organizations view customers as partners. Having a board of customers can be as important as a board of directors. Involving customers in every aspect of service—from creation to pricing to delivery to assessment—forges emotional connections. Alliance means union or joining. Its root word is "ally" from the French word meaning "to bind." And, the tie that binds in the world of service is an invitation to be a full member in the invention and formation of a service experience.

"If you can run the company a bit more collaboratively, you get a better result, because you have more bandwidth and checking and balancing going on."

—Larry Page, cofounder of Google

CHAPTER EIGHT

BE AS EASY AS A TV DINNER

"Focus on making it so easy for customers to do business with you that they will have little reason to look for greener pastures."
—Jill Applegate

We checked into the ranger's store to get our permit for a campsite. It was in the midst of a lush forest . . . especially the primitive area where we prefer to pitch our tent and build a campfire. As we were leaving the store to find our site, the receptionist said, "You might need this." It was what every Army infantry soldier would know as a P38—a miniature can opener.

We no doubt looked puzzled. "A can opener is the most frequently forgotten item, according to our campers," he explained. "We want your stay to be stress free!"

Customers are weary of stressful service. Lines like "Your call is very important to us," "We are experiencing unusual call volume," "Complete this form," "Please take a number," or "Did you have an appointment/reservation?" all signal dreaded effort, hassle, or frustration is on the other side. Some research shows that today effort (being easy to do business with) trumps every other feature of basic customer service.

Gourmet chefs, like gourmet service providers, "backward serve." They have a clear picture of what the preparation and presentation should be and then work backward from that goal to ensure the reality matches their vision. They also have a sixth sense for anticipating what can go wrong in service encounters. They know that it's not the lions and tigers that usually doom innovative service, it is the gnats and mosquitoes—those tiny irritants that are easy to overlook but often deliver pain or aggravation out of proportion to their size. To the customer, service hiccups are a lot like garlic. Never is there such a thing as a small amount.

A very gloomy *Wall Street Journal* on a very long flight left me with a very bad headache. And, I rarely get headaches! As soon as I exited the jetway at the San Francisco Airport, I headed for the nearest newsstand for some relief—Advil. I opened the plastic package and removed the two tablets in foil for some quick relief. Tucked behind the foil was a collapsible paper cup just big enough for two large swallows of water. What simple service innovation!

Stressless service starts with examining your customer's experience through their eyes. And, that often involves taking an "empathy walk" with customers because they see details we are blind to after we have worked for an organization about ninety days. It might involve calling your department, disguising your voice, and asking for something out of the ordinary to learn what your customers go through. It could include doing customer forensics by interviewing lost customers to uncover the real reasons they departed, not just what they said when they closed an account. It includes strongly encouraging complaints, keeping a log of concerns in order to spot trends, providing early warnings, or conducting root cause analysis to learn what creates customer disappointment and anxiety. And, in this era of self-service, it means ensuring there is always high touch along with high tech.

I recently watched three deer wander into my backyard. I live on the banks of a large lake. An inch of snow had made foraging for food more challenging for the deer, so they ventured beyond the woods nearby. They seemed cautious and quickly left without any attempt to find food. At first, I wondered why their short stay on this quiet, early morning. Then, it hit me! They were positioned between my house and the water with no woods at their back to scurry into should they encounter danger.

Customers are a lot like deer with no woods at their back. It explains the reason they get angrier than the situation dictates, or why they get very defensive when confronted with policies that make little sense to them. A self-service option can be great until it fails to work, leaving customers trapped. I watched a trucker at a roadside rest stop get a tire tool out of his rig and destroy a vending machine that kept his money and failed to dispense the beverage he selected. Service providers must never box customers into a corner without providing them outlets for escape should their experience turn anxious. Always give your customers woods at their back.

Are you a service provider who makes reaching a live person harder than winning the lottery? Is your service offering the only game in town—like a utility in some states? Do you hold your customers hostage with high switching costs or complicated account closing rules? If your customers call you, do you use your phone as an answering machine instead of an easy tool for two-way dialogue? Are you always reachable when your customers need you, or do you impose business hours convenient only to you? Is your self-service actually "you-are-entirely-on-your-own" service?

THE SECRET SAUCE—ACCESSIBLE

Twenty-four hour viruses are mystery bugs. Typically, you are totally clueless about where they come from or what makes them go away. All you know is that a 102-degree fever is not normal and medical help might be needed if you intend to not be slowed down by the malady!

It was 6:15 p.m. on a Sunday night, and I was flying to North Dakota on Monday to give a keynote. After enduring an afternoon of aches, I finally checked my temperature. I immediately called the Lake Oconee Urgent Care and got receptionist Christine. "You know we close in the summer at 6:30 p.m., but come on and we will get you in."

At 6:35, I walked in. Christine had already generated the paperwork and had an examining room on hold for me. With a twinkle in her eye, she asked if my birthdate had changed and what it was today. When I told her my birthdate, she smiled. "Yes, I have it here. I just wanted to make sure you were you and not someone else with your name!!"

After lots of questions and an examination, the physician assistant indicated a blood test was needed; seconds later, the nurse appeared. "Good evening, I'm Nurse Dracula here to take your blood." I laughed and started to feel better. At 6:55, I had a diagnosis, a prescription called in and waiting for me at the nearby pharmacy, and was all ready to leave. As I walked out, I heard the PA say, "Call me if you have concerns. And, break a leg in North Dakota tomorrow!"

We sometimes use medical service as a comical oxymoron—an example of poor service. At a time when we most have a need for speed and a desire for TLC, we sometimes endure long delays, cold examining rooms, arrogant medical professionals, disrespect for our temporary dependent state, and endless paperwork to satisfy the "rules r' us" insurance company or government.

It does not have to be that draconian. Make access to stressless service a vital and obvious part of your service recipe. After all, "stressed" spelled backwards is "desserts"!

"A nickel will get you on the subway,
but garlic will get you a seat."

—Old New York Proverb

CHAPTER NINE

BE THE ICING ON YOUR CUSTOMER'S CAKE

"Remarkable takes originality, passion, guts and daring . . .
today, the sure way to fail is to be boring."
—Seth Godin from *Purple Cow*

I was working with a client in Nicaragua. One evening, my business partner and I elected to skip the hotel grill and try the hotel's upscale restaurant—Factory Steak and Lobster. We were in for a special treat. I ordered my usual Jack Daniel's on the rocks. Now, in every restaurant in America such a request would yield a highball glass brought to the table already filled with ice plus the special adult beverage ready to drink. Because of that practice, I have gotten Jack poorly disguised as cheap bourbon, as well as a drink the bartender apparently measured with a thimble instead of a jigger.

But, at the Real Metrocentro InterContinental in Managua, I was not served Jack Daniel's, it was presented to me! The waiter brought a tray containing a full bottle of Jack, an empty chilled glass, a container of ice, and a tall shot glass. The glass was then filled with ice—one cube at a time—and placed before me. The bottle was presented much like a wine steward might present a chosen bottle of wine. Assuming approval, the Tennessee whiskey was poured into the shot glass that was then lovingly poured into the ice-filled highball glass! A simple shot of whiskey was treated like pricey Dom Perignon champagne.

Is your customer service like grape jelly? Now, don't get me wrong, I like grape jelly. And, you always get it with your toast or biscuit when you order breakfast at a restaurant . . . from the five-star gourmet type to the "what's a star?" truck stop. There is nothing bad about a customer experience that's like grape jelly—it's functional, ordinary, okeydokey kind of service. But, like grape jelly in a restaurant, it's not something customers would even mention. So, what if your service was more like strawberry-rhubarb jelly or prickly pear jelly?

Look for ways to make your service unique, novel, unusual, and out of the ordinary. What if the receipt was a sparkly color? What if the greeter was in costume, much like the bank that dressed lobby security guards like Wild West sheriffs? What if all the checkout clerks wore a funny hat every day, not just Halloween? What if the home page of your website had a treasure hunt, or contest, or game? What if the lobby counters in the hotel or bank had fun finger foods—like uniquely flavored jelly beans? What if you decorated the bathrooms with conversation-starting artwork? What if every customer left with a small souvenir? The options are as varied as the many flavors of jellies.

The chair was very unique in the pleasant, but largely functional, reception area. It was an intricately carved oak, straight-back chair. But what set it apart from all the other chairs and sofas was the fact that the chair's seat was upholstered in the cowhide of a Texas longhorn. The brown spots on the white background exactly matched the caramel-colored wood. It was the centerpiece of an experiment I talked my physician into trying. So, here is the backstory.

My physician was refurbishing the reception area of his relocated satellite office—the office nearest my home. I had given him a copy of my last book on innovative service, so he asked for my suggestions on the look of the reception area. "Why don't you make one chair significantly different from all the others? Put it within easy view of your receptionist and ask her to pay attention to how often that special chair is favored over all the other seats." He agreed. And, chose the cowhide-covered oak chair for his pilot.

Because I only see him a couple of times a year, I was eager to learn how his test turned out. "You were exactly right," he excitedly told me. "People picked that cowhide chair over ones that were clearly more comfortable. And, it proves your point: patients want a unique, off-the-beaten-path experience. I have already contacted my decorator to look for other ways we can create a special memory for our patients."

Now, he and I both know that one chair in one doctor's reception area does not a valid case make! Yet, it definitely gave him a new peephole into the potential of service with sprinkles. Plus, his new innovative service perspective freed him up to look for other applications. Try your own experiment. What could you do to make your customer's experience unexpectedly unique?

Is your service more like a light or more like a candle? It was the first thing that came to mind when I was asked by a radio host to characterize the difference between great service and innovative service. Lights are important because they provide us with the capacity to see (or see better). They help us traverse instead of stumble; read instead of squint; and be productive instead of lethargic. Candles do the same things, but with style. If you want a romantic dinner, you don't just turn on the light.

Great service is light-like; innovative service is candle-like. Both represent people doing their best to deliver an experience that delights customers. Spotlighted service builds loyalty; however, candlelit service creates advocacy. Lights are stable and bright; candles are shimmery and passionate. People who deliver great service focus on being good at what they do; people who deliver innovative service seek to add imagination to what they do.

I very much enjoy the consistency and focus on excellence found at most

Marriott hotels . . . from their squeaky clean rooms to their courteous front desk to their obvious zeal to be responsive to my needs. But, the Hotel Monaco leaves me with a story to tell . . . from their zebra or leopard print bathrobe in the closet to the goldfish in a bowl on my desk to the decor that makes me think I am a participant in a captivating tale. Next time you have an opportunity to shine a light on great service, try lighting your customer's candle instead! Oh, and please pass me the Grand Marnier Marmalade!!

THE SECRET SAUCE—ADVENTURE

I have a confession . . . I almost always go for the "off-the-beaten-path" choice. Tried and true is typically trumped by "I've never had that before." So you can imagine my reaction when the waiter seated us and handed us the breakfast menu with the announcement: "The buffet is a much better value than à la carte." But when he saw my nonplused reception he added, " . . . but none of the local flavors are on the buffet."

So, what did his announcement really mean? He meant that great food could be found on their standard value-added buffet—eggs (any style), bacon, sausage, pancakes, toast, pastries, fruit, yogurt, and cereal—everything you would want for a completely forgettable breakfast. And, the local flavors? This restaurant was on South Miami Beach, so it included Eggs Benedict Cubano, Caribbean French Toast, and Grilled Churrasco with hearth-fried eggs. Not exactly your everyday items, but clearly value-unique.

Innovative service is unexpected, off-the-beaten-path service. It delights because it is distinctive, not just excellent. It creates a story because it touches customers in ways "eggs and bacon" service can never do. But, just like "going with the local flavors" takes a willingness to be bold and daring, the return on investment can be well worth the road less traveled. Sometimes innovative service fails to please. And, there are customers who only want their service breakfast with "hash browns and toast."

Walk a bit on the wild side with your customers. Instead of recommending the predictable service buffet, deliver an experience more like ice-cold carrot juice with fresh ginger root! Take your customer on a memorable adventure and they will return with their fidelity and their funds.

"This is my advice to people: Learn how to cook, try new recipes, learn from your mistakes, be fearless, and above all have fun."

—Julia Child

FROM YOUR SERVICE KITCHEN TO YOUR CUSTOMER'S PLATE

"We dare not trust our wit for making our house pleasant to our friend, so we buy ice cream."
—Ralph Waldo Emerson

Ramen is a traditional Japanese noodle dish that, well prepared, is a highly desired delicacy. That's the backstory for the movie *The Ramen Girl*. A young woman finds herself in Tokyo and wants to understudy a master ramen chef who speaks no English; she speaks no Japanese. He's impatient and demanding; she works hard to be perfect. The climax of the movie (without giving away too much) happens when the frustrated chef takes his equally frustrated protégé to visit his mother, the person who taught him to be a great ramen chef.

Creating ramen, the mother tells the young woman, is not about mixing ingredients in the proper proportion and cooking the broth at the right temperature. In order to make a dish that connects your heart to your customer's heart, you must put your whole soul into the preparation and presentation, not just your smarts and sweat. It was a turning point. The woman let go of her pursuit of precision and embraced the "from the heart" expression of spirit. A recipe has no soul. As the chef of the service you deliver, you put in the heart and soul.

We have come to the end of our banquet of ideas for creating an unexpected, enchanting experience for those you serve. Thank you for joining. I hope it has been an inspiring, instructive experience for you. Innovative service takes you being a bold and fervent warrior in the war against boring and plain vanilla. As we take our final taste from this floating banquet we have shared, I leave you with an encouraging line by the imaginary chef Auguste Gusteau in the movie *Ratatouille* . . .

"You must be imaginative, strong-hearted.
You must try things that may not work, and you must not
let anyone define your limits because of where you come from.
Your only limit is your soul. What I say is true—anyone can cook . . .
but only the fearless can be great."

—Auguste Gusteau

ABOUT THE AUTHOR

Chip R. Bell is a senior partner with the Chip Bell Group and manages their office near Atlanta. A renowned keynote speaker, he has served as consultant, trainer, or speaker to such major organizations as GE, Microsoft, Nationwide, Marriott, Lockheed-Martin, Cadillac, KeyBank, Ritz-Carlton Hotels, United Technologies, Caterpillar, Eli Lilly, Verizon Wireless, USAA, Merrill Lynch, Hertz, Accenture, Cornell University, Harley-Davidson, and Victoria's Secret. Prior to starting a consulting firm in the early 1980s, he was director of Management and Organization Development for NCNB (now Bank of America). In 2014, The Chip Bell Group was ranked number six in North America among mid-sized consulting firms for leadership development. Additionally, Dr. Bell was a highly decorated infantry unit commander in Vietnam with the elite 82nd Airborne.

Chip is the author or coauthor of twenty books, many national and international bestsellers. Some of his previous books include *The 9½ Principles of Innovative Service, Wired and Dangerous* (coauthored with John Patterson and a winner of a 2011 Axiom Award as well as a 2012 Independent Publishers IPPY Award), *Take Their Breath Away* (also with John Patterson), *Managers as Mentors* (with Marshall Goldsmith and a winner of the Athena Award), *Magnetic Service* (with Bilijack Bell and a winner of the 2004 Benjamin Franklin Award), *Managing Knock Your Socks Off Service* (with Ron Zemke), *Service Magic* (also with Ron Zemke), *Dance Lessons: Six Steps to Great Partnerships* (with Heather Shea Schultz) and *Customers as Partners*. He has appeared live on CNBC, CNN, Fox Business Network, Bloomberg TV, NPR, ABC and his work has been featured in *Fortune, Businessweek, Forbes, Wall Street Journal,*

USA Today, Inc. Magazine, Entrepreneur Magazine, The CEO Magazine, WSJ MarketWatch, Leader to Leader, and *Fast Company.*

Chip can be reached at www.chipbell.com